SLOTHFUL: DOING NOTHING EXPECTING MUCH

IDENTIFYING AND OVERCOMING THE CURSE OF THE SLOTHFUL

AUDLEY REDWOOD

PREFACE
1. Poltergeist activity reveals curse of the slothful
2. Slothfulness keeps the believer from actively warring against sin
3. Slothful man lacks faith and patience
4. The way of a slothful man is as a hedge of thorns
5. A slothful man neglect his work
6. Breaking free to spiritual empowerment
7. Attainment of victory

Unless otherwise indicated the scriptural quotations are taken from the King James Version of the Bible.

Other reservoirs of information came from the Strong's Concordance and the NIV – New International Version used by the permission of Zondervan Publishing.
All rights Reserved
2nd Edition

Preface

The sole purpose of this book is to assist you in solving the most important issue you face: how to break free to spiritual empowerment so that you may begin to influence individuals and nations in your spiritual and social structure.

The topic with which I am introducing this series is called, the Curse of the Slothful. I have found out that most individuals mean well but do not know the strategies on which to begin their spiritual evaluation, transformation and restoration.

They have a sincere problem with recognizing the clear-cut method and the strategies necessary to bring spiritual reconciliation into their lives for freedom and empowerment.

This book is challenging, compelling with workable approaches that is genuinely helpful to bring about change.

CHAPTER ONE

The Poltergeist Activity Reveals Curse of the Slothful

It was about noontime when I heard cries of urgency coming from the upper end of the street where I stayed in the Island of Jamaica.

It was not uncommon to hear the voices of people in contention in that area of Kingston, the Island's capital. But this time, it was shouting that drew my attention so much so that my curiosity drew me pass the iron gated entrance to my home and out into the street where onlookers had started moving hastily in the direction towards the western corner of the block.

Therefore, as an inquisitive 13 years old, I lusted to see what was happening. Someone made mention that over in Asquith Street there was a sighting of a ghost (poltergeist) in the act of destroying one of the nearby residences. Suddenly, my attention was stirred and I decided to follow after the crowd in the direction of the poltergeist activity. I picked up the pace, determined that I would not miss out on anything for after all, incidences like this really happens.

From where I lived it was about a 200 yards to the point where the ghostly phenomenon was to shortly come to an end.

When I arrived at the location my attention was quickly drawn to the little house bordered by a 6 feet wooden fence and I noticed that everyone was on the opposite side of the street in an effort to stay back from the two-roomed house in which the event had occurred.

I also observed that there was an **atmosphere of perplexity** and from the tenants, fear and the shame of having their underhanded activity exposed in that they were dealings with satanic world and more so, to be found out to be not **masters of their craft**.

They were shown to be,
- a. Incompetent in their craft
- b. Lacking consistency in ordering their affairs
- c. Covenant breakers
- d. Deserving of their masters punishment

So now they stood there in the midst of all the spectators, with shame and terror on their faces wondering if being evicted by the **poltergeist activity** had been the end of their punishment.

The activity of a poltergeist is said to be a paranormal phenomenon, which alludes to the manifestation of an imperceptible entity. These imperceptible entities are in the habit of throwing objects about similar to what happened on Asquith Street.

The surmising of a 13-year-old boy was that the house, from which these individuals had been cast out, appeared as if the house furnishings had been completely destroyed by someone carelessly swinging a sledgehammer. The furnishings appeared to have been a complete disaster and evidently, it appeared as if during the process of reaping havoc on the dwelling that the terrified tenants had been forcibly thrown out through the windows and into the streets.

The curtain rods in the front room of the house hanged limply to the side of the window opening and there was no sign of the actual curtains. The windows on either side of the doorway were completely broken out with pieces of glass lying on the window ledge. The clothing and furniture were haphazardly thrown all about the home so that it gave rise to images of an **old cursed haunted house** in which human demolition had begun from the inside.

It's tenants were standing across the street, tattered, thorn and dispossessed of everything but their lives and the bare clothing on their backs. And now they were in trepidation for their lives not knowing whether their aggressors had concluded their onslaught or would return to finish the job.

As I reminisce over the event, I am reminded of the **sons of Sceva**, whom Paul called vagabond Jews and exorcist. Their father was highly esteemed in the community, as he was the chief of the Priest. With the father's religious estimation and may be political pull you can why his sons would also be highly regarded as exorcist among the common people.

When we speak of exorcism we are reminded of the movie called, The Exorcist, which was, a 1973 horror film directed by William Friedkin, and adapted by William Peter Blatty from his 1971 novel of the same name. In this film a demonically possessed child played by Linda Blair with (her dubbed voice came from Mercedes McCambridge) took center stage as the demon made a riot out of the catholic priest called in for the purpose of exorcism.

Exorcism is the driving out of evil spirits, which the exorcist believes will clear the mind of oppressive feeling and relating demonic activity.

The word has its root in the word **"exit"** which means departure or a means of leaving a place.

In the event noted in the **Book of Acts 19:14**, Sceva's seven sons had been faced with a demoniac and instead of going to the proper source to get the job done, willfully tried exorcism on their own by using the incantation, ***"in the name of the Lord Jesus whom Paul preaches"***. At that, the demon spoke up and said, "Jesus I know, Paul I know but who are you?

When the demon doesn't know his opponent that means he has sniffed around your atmosphere and cannot find you as a notable contender because only those who are washed in the blood of Jesus can be classed as notable contenders for their names are written in the Lambs Book of Life.

A demonic entity must be able to find your **connection with the blood of the Lord Jesus** who Paul made it clear in Colossians 2:15 that the Lord

"… *having spoiled principalities and powers, he made a show of them openly, triumphing over them in it*"

You will always be triumphant with the blood of Jesus for there is no enemy that can withstand a man or woman dressed in the full armor of God and washed in the blood. But the sons of Sceva contended from their **own weaknesses and not from the strength of the risen Christ** and so were domed to failure from the very beginning. Paul says in 1Cor. 2:4 that his speech and his preaching was not with enticing words of mans wisdom, but in **demonstration of the Spirit and of power**. Therefore, God has given every born-again believer power and authority over all the powers of the enemy and nothing shall by any means harm them. But this power works for those who are in alignment with God and not for those who would use it presumptuously. It is Satan's job to tempt you into doing presumptuous acts for which the grace of Lord God is not liable for they do not give honor and glory to God but to man. To try to exorcise a demon in your own strength is similar to foolishly playing with a deadly snake and presumptuously using the word of God for a defense when bitten, it will not work.

Therefore, what the sons of Sceva required was a **resignation from self-will** to become **enlisted with the army of Lord** so that the power of the resurrection life brought forth by the blood of Jesus might have free course to work in their lives to glorify the living God.
Scripture declares that **the man, whom the evil spirit possessed, jumped on them** and overpowered them all. He gave them such a beating that they ran out of the house naked and bleeding.

But at Asquith Street my curiosity was short lived for I had come to witness an ongoing demonic manifestation and had seen no such thing only the result of it. In my teenage mind, I considered this event not at all a complete loss of time for at least on my return to school I would have had a story to tell and with a few exaggerations, I would definitely gain an audience, maybe even a free lunch from my classmates.

This also goes to show why it is expedient that we as parents intercede for a defense for our children minds to block out every ungodly and false word that they would otherwise indiscriminately give ear. It is important that we surround our children with faith filled words that gives the Spirit of God room to operate in their hearts and minds and to know that they are kept by those same prayers while they are away from our homes.

Nevertheless, we all stood by looking at the house at which the paranormal phenomena took place hoping that by some strange mental phenomena we could force a part two but there was no such manifestation. The demons had concluded their activity and as **trained dogs** sent to do their master's bidding, they had taken the spoil and returned from whence they came.

The victims had fallen headlong into a "**Curse**" and as a young boy, though not able to put it all in perspective, yet I immediately saw the **image of a curse**.

As I retraced my steps to my house I wondered about what I had just seen and wondered at the loss brought upon the lives of these people by these invisible creatures.
While I was at the scene of the **poltergeist manifestation** someone had mentioned the name, "Delawrence", and that this "Delawrence" was said to be a man who studied the science of divination and had been responsible for administration of this terrible loss. There had however been a reason for this satanic judgment. For it seemed the occupants had reneged on paying their part on some attained satanic privilege.

Principle: the undeserved curse doesn't come to rest

The KJV put it like this in proverb 26:2,
"*As the bird by wandering, as the swallow by flying, so the curse causeless shall not come*".

Therefore, as a young boy it became obvious that a curse doesn't come unless there is a cause. I saw that there was an apparent "**broken covenant**". The owners of the house had signed a contract with the **"destroyer"** and after they had received the **"benefits"** of the contract had forgotten that there was a price to be paid. The scripture tells us to swear to your own hurt and fail not to comply with covenantal decree. These words bare relevancy in all areas of human life.

Principle: Swear to your own hurt and changeth not.

But we see that these individuals had not **given much weight to or procrastinated** and so failed to keep their end of the covenant they had made with evil. I realize then that the enemy will make it is so easy to attain the most unattainable but at what price? Are you willing to put a price on your soul for material gain?

Doing business with the enemy is a practice done in most third world nations and as always the pawn is so taken up by the effortless industrial and personal benefits that he doesn't pay attention to the **balloon notes** that never ends. The enemy is an acute businessman who sells a wrapped package of bondage, evil desires in lovely beautifully designed and handsomely craft and detailed venues of operation. But the destruction to those who buy his wares is everlasting bondage except by mercy, God accepts a remorseful plea for salvation and grants repentance through the shed blood of his Son, the Lord Jesus.

Therefore, the enemy's dramatic display of evil is never merciful when it comes to the forgiveness of debts. Therefore making a covenant with evil will always result in a **climatic tragedy of grief** for the enemy has no mercy on those who are found to be laid-back, lethargic or lazy when their part of the agreement is not kept.

Principle: **You cannot play by the devil's rules and expect to win.**

While at the scene as bystander to this occurrence of poltergeist activity, I realized that if ever I looked at a curse, this was one. Surely, the material positions could be replaced but what was the condition of the soul? Had they signed the doted line or was there yet hope for deliverance and restoration from this terrible blight-like experience? Yet, for now, I was beholding the extent of a curse of one who was **slothful in paying his "debts" to his unmerciful master who had come and taken all that he had**. He had purposely made a show of the occupants openly to assert his lordship over their lives and to attach a spirit of fear to prevent any future failure to meet his demands. The poltergeist activity now made everyone aware that to fall under the control of the enemy was to fall under the control of a curse.

CHAPTER TWO

Slothfulness Keeps the Believer from Actively Warring Against Sin

In the book of 2 Samuel there is a story of an affair that has had sordid historical consequences, resulting in both the loss of self-esteem and loss of life. The story gives us five main players; David, the incumbent king, Bathsheba, the wife of Uriah, Joab, the son of David's sister Zeruiah and general of David's army and Nathan the prophet.

Now Bathsheba was the daughter of Eliam from the town of Giloh and the supposedly granddaughter of Ahithophel who was David's councilor until he betrayed him to join forces with Absalom, who was to attempt a take-over of his father's house.

They had been prominent citizens, noting the closeness to the palace and the reputation of Ahithophel as a sagacious councilor.

The Executive Decision

Now it was the time of the year when Kings go out to war but David, the Jewish king, made a decision to send his general. In those days, it was the custom for the king to lead their armies into battle, noting the spiritual and emotional significance. But David, now being influenced by the spirit of slothfulness, made an unorthodox decision to remain at home.

It's important that we understand that David's "executive decision", without divine counseling **to be at ease in Zion,** was at the wrong season, for he allowed spiritual laxity to become an opportunist when it was time for war.

Just as in the days of David, so is it now, for God is asking, where are my 'kings" – Why aren't they in spiritual warfare?

- A servant is incapable of doing some assignments given specifically to a "king".

A king makes decrees and the servant follow the decrees made by the king. We fall into the error of believing that some one else can do our **God ordained assignments**. Slothfulness deceives us into thinking that another "family member" will serve the divine purpose for which God has ordained you.

David knew of the skill set of his sister's son Joab, and felt safe sending him out to do the king's assignment.

But what David failed to understand was that the God of Israel neither slumbers nor sleeps. Besides, his thoughts are far above man's thoughts; and his ways are far above anything that man could imagine (Isa.55:8).

- **David wanted to make judgments and decisions for God**.

What the Mighty God was saying was that if I, the Most High wanted to send a "**Joab**", then a "**Joab**" I would have anointed and not a "**David**". The Lord God was implying that, I the Lord **know what's best for my people Israel**. God was saying, David, you might have been a shepherd over a few sheep but I am the **Chief Shepherd** of my people Israel.

God is saying that, I am the Good Shepherd and the divine Commander of all the earth and it is I who has given you oversight of all Israel, **to physically lead them into battle**. God was saying, do you think it was a mistake when I anointed you to slay the bear and the lion?

He is saying, David I was setting you up for a ministry!

- **The point here was that God, in his divinity, choose David and David in his carnality choose Joab.**

Principle: God always gets the glory out of his choice but what man chooses, the glory goes to man.

Man can choose someone but if man's choice cannot **identify with none of your needs,** then what good is he? What good is it if the one man chooses is without the God given anointing to breakthrough for a breach in the enemy's camp? It's the anointing that breaks the yolk and God gives special anointing to those he has chosen in a location, time and a season.

Therefore you want to be chosen by one who has a **providential perspective**; one who can supply all your needs according to his riches in glory by Christ Jesus.

Know Where You Fit

The enemy had run interference with his relationship with God; he had become lax in his spiritual walk and so David was doing what was convenient to his flesh rather than being connected to the ordinances of God. Therefore his spiritual relationship was strained and as a king, a strained relationship will always lead "king" into **a place of uncertainty**.

The man anointed of God, had allowed the spirit of Slothfulness to hinder him from fulfilling what was divinely appointed for, "*it was a time when kings go out to war*" but David sent Joab instead.

When there is an anointing for a given assignment yet one fail to enter into this assignment, one border on rebellion. David disobeyed on **ongoing statute**, that is, it was wartime, and a king was expected to go out of his comfort zone and out into the fields where God had chosen the war to be fought. These are the days when the saints of God prefer the luxury and the comfort of the world than the challenges that is faced to liberate them that are bound by the tyranny of this world. The spirit called Slothfulness will lead you into the way of your uncommon weakness instead of uncommon valor.

David knew that it was the season when kings go out to war, and he knew that God had anointed him, to **capture new territories and the restoration of lands** that had been given to Abraham's descendants. He knew that he was the choice man for the job and so his fight was in the **interest of God**. But he had allowed slothfulness to set in and the Set-Man was quickly losing ground.

The influence of the spirit of Slothfulness has been acknowledged as one of the spirits in operation when a Believer, for the sake of **convenience and comfort**, neglects his sanctified duty in the house of the Lord giving it to another of unqualified spiritual identity. Therefore this shows the influence of the **spirit of slothfulness** upon the king, for he now places little value on,

- **The mercies and the grace of God upon his life**
- The anointing for **divine empowerment**

David, under the **influence of unseen spiritual warfare**, and made the unqualified decision that rather than being in the presence of the Ark where the God of Israel was awaiting his voice, he would rather be in the shadows of comfort and luxury.

You see what David failed to understand was that it was the duty of the king to "fight first" before the actual fighting begun on the battlefield. It is the duty of the king to "**withstand**' first, to set-up the strategies that he will receive from God before he "**stands**" on the battlefield. It is that time when the fight is won in the spirit so that your army, in the midst of the battlefield, may stand with boldness as you wait for your manifested victory.

It is not unlike believers, who instead of going to intercessory prayer at their local church, would rather remain home and deny God their voice upon the earth. Therefore his people are kept in captivity because those who have been given some light refuse to allow those in darkness become enlightened. They refuse to be involved in prayer, not by presumptuous sin but by the enemy's deception that having a more expensive car, house and jewelry is a better witness for God than the sacrifice of prayer.

The tricks of the enemy are endless; he is a deceiver and sometimes he will whisper into your mind and he will say, "You don't have to war today, allow someone else in your place, after all, you have already slain your "Goliath". Besides, "Joab" can do an excellent job. So go ahead and take off today".

But he is concealing the spiritual dynamics in operation, for it was not **Joab's presence** that was in demanded here but **David's anointing**!

David Extreme Desire

The result of David's slothfulness was the lusting after Bathsheba. The story implies that David lusted when he looked at Mrs. Bathsheba's physical "afro-centricity". The book of James unreservedly tells us,

"But every man is tempted, when he is drawn away of his own lust, and enticed. Then when lust hath conceived, it bringeth forth sin: and sin, when it is finished, bringeth forth death." Ja.1:14, 15

This **event, which was unusual for a king of David's caliber**, occurred while Bathsheba washed in her own private bathing compartment that was situated on the rooftop area of her house.

The proximity to the king's house leads us to imply that her family was of considerable means. The balcony of the palace overlooked the dwellings in the city and so the king had a clear view of what was supposed to be a private occasion. But when you are not at your assigned location then the enemy is at his strongest in his attacks against you. Things that were previously hidden, things which the angels of God had been keeping under concealment to **protect you're anointing**, they will now become apparent because your guard has been taken down.

- **The devil is always on the prowl as a roaring lion to set you up to become a curse**.

That is why some images are best to remain unseen because God knows **the impact it will have upon your spirit**. The weapon of the enemy of using the female gender as been used ever since the dawn of man and regrettably has had much success in the destruction of families, the splitting of churches and even wars between nations.

We see in the book of Job, there is a deterrent to illegal contact between the sexes. Job gives this statement of which heed should be given, he says, "*I have made a covenant with mine; why then should I think upon a maid?* Another translation says, "I made a covenant with my eyes **not to look with lust** at a young woman'. NLT Job knew that it was easy to fall into the devil's trap when we gaze upon a woman without having proper certification.

- **That's why some hidden things must remain unrealized until it is the will of God to reveal a matter.**

Therefore, while surveying the holy city from his balcony king David had a revealing image of Uriah's wife, which stirred his emotions with an uncontrollable desire to be with her. The resultant actions would prove that he was unable to deal responsibly with what he had seen.

The intentions of his heart, as **he glared upon the nudity** of Bathsheba, had caused him to become temporarily separated from his God. The king was unable to keep his composer, for he was taken by her apparent beauty and **without thinking about the consequence of his action,** he sent for the woman in secret.

The king knew that what he had stumbled upon was **morally incorrect** but the beauty of the man's wife had surfeited his appetite, and so the king became a captive of lust. Under the cover of the now **darkness of his mind,** he expected to play the devil's game and win.

The vanity of beauty has captivated men, even from the Garden of Eden and now this king, unable to control his appetite, went beyond his boundaries and driven by lust, the king made a "demand" upon the wife of Uriah who had no choice but to submit.

- **He was king, and she was only the wife of a Hittite, the descendant of Heth, a most valiant and honorable man.**

Therefore the value that was placed upon her would be far less than that of a true Israelite woman. What I mean is she was not believed to be a descendant of Abraham and except for her salacious beauty would have borne a second class status in the Judaic culture. Yet David had little regard for Bathsheba class or race, he wanted only to be satisfied by that exceptionally erotic image that he had seen on the rooftop. He was a man trapped within the carnality of his soul, a prisoner of an image which he was bound to until his release.

David stood under the condemnation of his own law but he could care less, for now lust had to be hastily conceived. The devil didn't remind him nor was it his job to remind him, that lust, would bring forth sin: and sin, when it was finished, **would bring forth the death of Uriah and the child that was conceived.**

- **The Devil will pocket everyone who makes a decision to play his game**

Therefore, when the act was over and the manifestation began to take shape, David, under the weakness of a mere man, strategically improvised a method of denial. So when he discovered the pregnancy of Bathsheba, he sent a message to Joab, who was now taking David's place on the battlefield, to **send Uriah the Hittite home.**

On Uriah's arrival at the palace, he was debriefed as to the condition of the armed forces. David's plan of having Uriah to go into his wife so Uriah would be the father of David's child seemed to be working exactly as he had planned. The king sent one of his servants to Uriah to say how he had greatly pleased the king; hence the king would like to reward him for being such a skilled, talented and brave soldier with time spent with his wife.

Therefore, he said, go home to your wife and spend some rest and relaxation with her. But Uriah, being a man sworn to duty and a man of integrity pleaded with the king asked for he would not be given to indulgence while his fellow soldiers were being killed in battle. He said to the king 2Sam.11:11,

"The ark, and Israel, and Judah, abide in tents; and my lord Joab, and the servants of my lord, are encamped in the open fields; shall I then go into mine house, to eat and to drink, and to lie with my wife? As thou livest, and as thy soul liveth, I will not do this thing".

David Reaction to Uriah

The urgency of the situation became overwhelming after hearing **Uriah's resolute response**. Here was a **Hittite** who showed more honor to the God of Israel than the king whom he had chosen, for he recognized that,

- He **needed to be in the presence of the Ark** of the Covenant.
- He needed to be where God had chosen to be.
- He knew that the blessing comes from following after God
- He knew the expediency of bringing timely destruction to the enemy
- He knew that it was not God's perfect will for the Ark to be in open fields

Uriah's Integrity

Uriah was exhibiting submission, humility and honor to Israel's God. He was expressing faithfulness and loyalty while David had expressed weakness for the possession that he held. Yet Uriah did not come to his king with a railing accusation but he afflicted himself by saying, "The ark, and Israel, and Judah abide in tents; shall I then go into mine house, and eat, and drink and lie with my wife? In other words, he was saying as David when he had a zeal for God, "Is there not a cause?

David plans could not stand against the honor that Uriah had for the God of Israel. His hope to get Uriah drunk so that he may change his mind under the influence of strong drink and go lay with his wife had failed. **Uriah would not be swayed for he held on to his integrity and he knew that it was better to please God than man**.

Finally, the king wrote a letter to Joab who he had placed over Israel's army, saying, ***"Set ye Uriah in the forefront of the hottest battle, and retire ye from him, that he may be smitten, and die".***

David uncovered Uriah's nakedness by sleeping with his wife then committed the fatal sin and murdered him. Hence the king, not having the **technological skills** in those days to perform an abortion and seemingly left with no other choice that would cover his adultery, was deceived into yet another trap, to send Uriah back to the front lines and have him murdered. His plans were carried out and when the woman's husband was murdered, the cover-up continued as he took her to wife.

A curse doesn't come without a cause and the cause in this biblical text was that David was out of place. It was a time when kings go out to war but one king in particular, showed sign of weakness; he was slothful and it was to cost him exceedingly.

David's Secret Uncovered

After about 2 years, God sent Prophet Nathan to David with an allegory. He said, **2 Samuel 12**:

¹ The LORD sent Nathan to David. When he came to him, he said, "There were two men in a certain town, one rich and the other poor. ² The rich man had a very large number of sheep and cattle, ³ but the poor man had nothing except one little ewe lamb he had bought. He raised it, and it grew up with him and his children. It shared his food, drank from his cup and even slept in his arms. It was like a daughter to him.

⁴ "Now a traveler came to the rich man, but the rich man refrained from taking one of his own sheep or cattle to prepare a meal for the traveler who had come to him. Instead, he took the ewe lamb that belonged to the poor man and prepared it for the one who had come to him."

[5] David burned with anger against the man and said to Nathan, "As surely as the LORD lives, the man who did this must die! [6] He must pay for that lamb four times over, because he did such a thing and had no pity."

David was **repulsed** by the sayings of Nathan and his reaction was explosive with anger. What man would dare do such a **wicked and merciless thing**?

He could **identify** with the poor man and his sheep because before God anointed him to be king he was the least of Jesse's sons. His job was **watching the sheep**, protecting them from every adversary who as is mentioned came in to prey upon his sheep as a lion and the bear. He knew the helpless nature of a sheep and the security and the calm assurance they were given when someone was standing by them not only with a **rod and a staff** but cared for them.

It was David who had penned the **23rd Psalms** which began with the banner declaration that "the Lord is my

Shepherd, I shall not want" and from this David knew that sometimes the "**sheep would have unforeseen accidents and misfortunes**", falling into pits and getting sick because of their inability to relate to their environment. Nevertheless, it was the shepherd's job to care for his sheep, and pounding them for unforeseen accidents was never justified. Extreme waywardness of a sheep required extreme attention but that was done out of love for the sheep so that the shepherd always remained merciful to the sheep.

David had been a **good shepherd** for a good shepherd would give his life in the protection of his sheep. He had been tested before with **the lion and the bear** that had came against his sheep and had passed his test with flying colors by destroying both of them.
Notice it did not say that he wounded them but that he **destroyed them or he made an end of their ministry**. Today we are not called to wound satanic strongholds but to destroy them.

David had been known to be a good shepherd because he had the ability to meet the **practical needs of his sheep**. But when **he was influenced** by the **spirit of slothfulness** in the **office of a king**, he became selfish and took the life of the poor man's "sheep" rather than give his own.

- **Slothfulness attempts to make one powerless to fight so that one yields to temptation and ultimately is lured into bondage.**

So God sent the **prophet Nathan** to make plain to the king that his deception, murder, insensitivity, and holding Bathsheba against her will and adultery. The fact that he had committed iniquity against his sheep and against God had not gone unnoticed.

Principle: **God's word will always take you back to the "place of identity" or the place where you strayed from your purpose before you are allowed to proceed to the place of revelation.**

It was after then that David in remorseful repentance penned Psalms 51 because of the aggregate of sins brought on by one **act of slothfulness**. How David repented of his failure to go out to war where the God of Israel had been awaiting on his appearance instead of remaining at home to have a devilish deception run its course. **During these economic times, it becomes fertile ground for the spirit of slothfulness to operate**.

Economic Destitution

The **first apparent reason** for the progress of slothfulness is economic devastation. Man is laboriously trying to get ahead for the betterment of his home and family only to find that the opportunities are meager and that there is no apparent hope of change.

Secondly, they fail to **identify** with and pray God's word and end up regretting their once hopeful lives. Often the failure of success of any family is the failure to pray and believe God's word.

Many people are **influenced by the dark forecast** issued over the multiplicity of media arrangements and this in turn gives a dark outlook on their personal lives.

We can only guess at what David's forecast had been. We know it was a time when kings go off to war against the enemy that would try to **overshadow the presence of God's people** and David refused to fight.

In essence, David told the God,

 "**No, I will not go and take territories for your kingdom**".

David was neglecting the investment God had made in his life by denying God a successful operation on the battlefield. **One man can make a difference because he is the one who carries the anointing** to be king and to lead God's "army" into battle. Because God's anointed man is not in a place then destruction can be the result. David was God's set-man and you can only have one set-man at a time. In other words, God knows that anything with two heads is a monster and he does not call monsters to bear rule over his kingdom.

Therefore, it was a time when the anointing of the set man was required for victory to be achieved. It is God's anointing that he put on the set man. It is God who gives it and requires obedience that the anointing on the set man might flourish. Hence the anointing will break the yolk and the presence of God will reign. Wherever you find the anointing you will find fertility and with fertility comes reproduction.

The spirit of slothfulness will try to make a leprechaun out of your desire to become a success and overcome the changes brought on by every day living. We note here that a leprechaun is short and can never reproduce.

Slothfulness is a spirit that seeks to stop your ability to have positive successful spiritual reproduction.
You must be able to reproduce, to create new life not just to see the situation and make fun of your disparity because of your seemingly inability to create change.

Slothfulness eats away at your confidence, your faith and your energy that you need to carry on through to victory. The Bible says in Daniel 7:25 that the adversary, *"... Shall speak great words against the most high, and shall wear out the saints of the most high..."*

People have become so **overcome by slothfulness** that their once **emerging lives** tend to become **valueless and stuck in the wall called mediocrity**.

But God says,
"*Lift up your head, O ye gates, Be lifted up ye ancient doors, so that the king of glory may come in*" (Psalms 24:9).
God wants to come into our lives and reign gloriously that we will have no need to be affected by the spirit of slothfulness but we must have among other things,

    a. **An open ear**
    b. A **discerning spirit**.

But we see that the **slothfulness** in king David's life prevented him from **hearing the voice of the Lord** and for 2 years since the occurrence of the event with **Bathsheba he lived an un-submissive life**.

Too many of us are going around with a rebellious and disobedient spirit functioning in our religious services with no anointing. You see, we left communicating with the holy God some time ago and so we are going about on the fumes of our pass anointing.

The saints of the living God knows us by **our names** because of what we did, **all our victories are past tense** but we have nothing to show for the present because our leaves have become dry and there is no victory in our voices.

Our prophetic words have become more like "**pathetic words**" because there is no revelation only past memories and experiences. We give a word based upon appearance for if Bro. Joe appears wealthy this week we will say wealth has come into your life O man, and if he appears poor next week we say, "I curse the spirit of poverty on your life". Thus the spirit of slothfulness has given rise to a familiar spirit and **we cannot recognize that we are in need of revival**.

Ever since the event with Bathsheba, David must have sensed the **lack of communication** between God and himself. Nothing could be done to placate this feeling of emptiness, which brought about concealed condemnation and guilt.

I am unaware of any person in God's kingdom who have not fallen under condemnation, but some of us are quick to repent, plead the blood and with boldness, return to a overcoming life. Others allow the noise of the world, and the situations that came with the condemnation to hold them captive from seeking God for repentance, so they could live a life of victory. Believers must become aware that God unmistakably said through the Apostle Paul, that

*"There is therefore now **no condemnation**, which are in Christ Jesus, who walk not after the flesh, but after the Spirit.*
For the law of the Spirit of life in Christ Jesus hath made me free from the law of sin and death.
For what the law could not do, in that it was weak through the flesh, God sending his own Son in the likeness of sinful flesh, and for sin, condemned sin in the flesh: *that the righteousness of the law might be fulfilled in us, who walk not after the flesh, but after the Spirit."*
Romans 8:1- 4

If you continue to walk after the flesh then sin is not condemned for you

Diligence

The dictionary gives these meanings for the word "diligence",
1. Persistent effort
2. Legal carefulness

Other words used in its description are: meticulousness, industry, thoroughness, assiduousness, conscientiousness, attentiveness and carefulness.

It is no need to ask how diligent we are in the word and prayer, for if it is in the root it will be in the fruit. Is there a spiritual famine in the land?

What a glorious day it will be when all the children of God will lay aside their pride and begin in one accord to walk in a **spirit of repentance** and to ask the Lord our God for wisdom so that we may know how to be **diligent in all that we have been called**. Slothfulness and diligence can never be in synchrony and so the believer who allows the spirit of a sloth to hamper his life is spiritually weak, slow and tardy.

David, Where Are You?
The king knew of his strained relationship with God. He knew that he was undergoing a guilt complex but as long as on the external everyone pretended that it was not a problem then he was able to live with what he had done but he knew that God was not pleased. God had chosen David, and his chastisement would come from God and not man. He knew that the situation between Bathsheba and him had hardly been put to rest and that one-day he would have to pay the consequence for his sin. Therefore he expected the Lord's verdict but he did not know the hour or the day, but like judgment day, he was certain of its coming.

Here we see a problem in leadership and that the king was accountable to none and the elders in his court dare not stand up and tell the king that he had committed adultery and now was seeking to commit fratricide. After all, they wanted to continue to be in good terms with the king even at the risk of their integrity. And so, a leader who is surrounded by a group of "yes-men" will soon loose his ship for lack of astute council. Hence, when the ship is sunk, the "yes-men" like a bunch of rats, will all swim ashore or to another vessel to become "yes-men" all over again.

David Had A Suddenly Moment
Suddenly, God sent Nathan to visit David to make him aware of an atrocity that took place in his kingdom. Nathan waited until David heard the entire story and in outrage gave his judgment. Suddenly, Nathan then told the king that he was the man in his allegory and that the child would have no future.

The child would never reign as king neither would the king be able to watch him grow into a young man so that he could cultivate in him the wisdom of the God of Israel. This regrettable situation happened all because of the influence of a slothful spirit.

A word from a **set person** in your life will always bring about the needed change because of its **revelation content**. So as David heard the word, he cries out for repentance and that the life of the child would be spared. But I believe that David, as much as he knew God, **knew that the child had been living on borrowed time**. I believe that David's major cry was for that intimate relationship he once had with the Holy Spirit.

His sin was a blatant disregard of God's sovereignty. He was the first priest-king ordained by God to have a seed that would forever be on the throne of Israel. He was called a man after God's own heart and yet he foolishly allowed the enemy to work in his nature. He pleaded for restoration.

We feel the burden of his loss and the urgency of his cry for restoration inked in Psalms 51 which begin as he prays, *"Have mercy upon me, O God, according to thy loving-kindness: according to thy tender mercies, blot out my transgression"*.

Even though the king must have made a sin sacrifice, the memory of the offense still remained with him because in his mind the blood of Uriah cried out from the ground. Only the blood of Jesus could justify and cleanse the sins that David had committed. Only the blood of the lamb could give perfect peace. Isaiah says that the chastisement of our peace was upon Him and with His stripes we are healed. This we know for the blood of bull and goats cannot take away sin but merely atone for them. In other words it made up for the misdeed until the true sacrifice was given.

God retained the memory for when David asked God for permission to build the temple (1Chron.28: 3), God remembered the blood in David's life and that he had been a man of war and denied him that opportunity.

Only the blood of the Lord Jesus Christ has the power to blot out sin.
David's heart needed to be cleaned up from spiritual filthiness. He had needed **to remove the shed blood of**

Uriah from his hands on account of the spirit of slothfulness.

The sin of slothfulness was not only occasioned to David's day but to ours as well. **In David's case his temptation came in an "exotic bundle" on top of Uriah's roof**. What will be the shape or form of your slothfulness when it comes? What is the area of your weakness?

Today, technology has made the earthly expense of a sinful lifestyle to appear bearable and without shame. Besides, the scenario between today's "Bathsheba and David" comes in a multiplicity of seduction arrangements. This comes with the false hope afforded by science of several quick fix options and so the breaking of God's commandments bares little revelance on our society.

Scientific Deception

But what science has not told us is that "Bathsheba's" physical health is at stake. Medical science has not amplified the consequences of the seduction but wants us to believe that after she has been seduced into sin all that's necessary is that she makes a short visit to the doctor's office to get an abortion. It doesn't tell her about the lifetime of loneliness that awaits her.

It doesn't tell her that she might never be able to hear the words, "Mama" coming from her own child because of a one night out with the "dogs", which ended up in a physical affair and pregnancy.

Today's "Bathsheba" is under the supposition that a short visit to the abortion clinic would be the solution but nobody told her that there was a risk of destroying her fallopian tube or **her stomach lining pulled** out as the operating physician destroys the unknown soul.

Science is silent about the topic of abortion because society sees it as all a big game. And no one mentions the fact that just maybe the abortion clinics share the responsible of not educating "Bathsheba" enough before the actual abortion is done. However, if the mother knew the dangers she might have to endure then you would scarcely see as many abortions as we have seen knowing the complications that were possible on the operating table.

But as long as this "preferential slothfulness" continues, "Bathsheba's" will have no voice.

For the "David's" of today, repentance and forgiveness must be made. It needed the blood of Jesus and not blood of bulls and goats to remove the chastisement for David's peace, which included the removal of two years worth of "decaying demonic feces" from his mind.

I want you to get an image of your spiritual house being inhabited by demonic rodents-like creatures for 2 years. Imagine the eaten up walls and floors, furniture eaten up with claw prints with a covering of excrement and the worst lingering odor in which you ever came into contact, all this is a symbolic representation of the **spirit of slothfulness**.

Let us pray:

Father we thank you for the blood of Jesus that covers our thoughts and our minds keeping us from every spirit of slothfulness.

We thank you that the blood covers my doorpost and every possession and position that you have given me.

We thank you for the shield of faith that has protected us from every wandering thought that has been sent by the enemy to create negative mental images.

We thank the Lord that we have been given boldness to enter the presence of God through the blood.

We thank the Lord that we have received the fullness of the Holy Spirit and because of the blood we can say that the spirit of Slothfulness has no part in us.

Chapter Three

Slothful Man Lacks Faith and Patience

Let me begin by saying that every believer is blessed for which the Apostle Paul gives us evidence in the Book of Galatians. He says that,

"Christ hath redeemed us from the curse of the law, being made a curse for us: for it is written, Cursed is every one that hangeth on a tree: that the blessing of Abraham might come on the Gentiles through Jesus Christ; that we might receive the promise of the Spirit through faith." (3:13-14)

Every believer then has received the promise of the Spirit through faith in God. This is witnessed in Acts 2:38 where

Peter addressed an audience of Jews who came to celebrate Pentecost. At that time the city of Jerusalem was stirred to its core and many received the message of Christ and Christ crucified. The Apostle Peter made it plain onto them, that if they repent and be baptized they would receive the gift of the Holy Spirit which God had promised. During his message three thousand souls were saved believing that they had been redeemed from the curse of the law and that now they had received the blessings of Abraham though faith.

What are the blessings of Abraham?

The bible tells us that Abraham believed God and it was counted unto him for righteousness. In other words, Abraham had faith in God to fulfill what the Lord had promised. So in Genesis 12:1-3 we take a look at seven blessings given to Abraham. The scripture list them as,

1. I will lead you unto a land that I will show thee, Gen.12:1
2. I will make of thee a great nation, Gen.12:2
3. I will bless thee, Gen.12:2
4. I will make thy name great, Gen.12:2

5. I will make thee a blessing, Gen. 12:2
6. I will bless them that bless thee, Gen. 12:3
7. In thee all the families of the earth shall be blessed, Gen. 12:3

Now it's important that you keep in mind Galatians 3:14, which says,

"That the blessing of Abraham might come upon the Gentiles through Jesus Christ; that we might receive the promise of the Spirit through faith".

Seeing then that we have such a great High Priest who liveth to make intercession for our souls, where then does the curse of slothfulness appear? Does it appear because of misuse of the liberty we have been given?

Paul says, "**But take heed lest by any means this liberty of yours become a stumbling block to them that are weak".**

For if any man see thee which hast knowledge sit at meat in the idol's temple, shall not the conscience of him which is weak be emboldened to eat those things

which are offered to idols, And through thy knowledge shall the weak brother perish, for whom Christ died?

But when ye sin so against the brethren, and wound their weak conscience, ye sin against Christ.

Wherefore, if meat make my brother to offend, I will eat no flesh while the world standeth, lest I make my brother to offend. (1Cor.8:9-13)

In other words, watch your influence because lack of proper influence will lead some brethren to spiritual inactivity which leads to a decrease in their faith level.

Remember our walk is by faith and emptiness is the result little faith which offers a resting station for doubt and unbelief. The enemy looks for those who because of doubt have no spiritual intensity, no passion and no zeal for God and his **word**.

The Psalmist says, "***Thy word is a lamp unto my feet, and a light unto my path***". (119:105) But when there is no word to feed your spirit and to give intensity to your faith then it won't be long before one becomes increases in slothfulness and a **slothful life is a staggered life, filled with uncertainty**.

Therefore, inactivity in the word, if not prevented, will lead to a spirit of slothfulness.

In the book of Hebrews 6:11-12 the Apostle encourages the believers, he says,
"And we desire that every one of you do shew the same diligence to the full assurance of hope unto the end: **that ye be not slothful**, *but followers of them who through faith and patience inherit the promises.'*

This word "slothful" comes from the Greek word **"nothros"** *no-thros'* **sluggish**, that is (literally) *lazy*, or (figuratively)*:* —dull, slothful (dim, thick, dense, slow, brain-less). Strong's Dictionary

Apostle Paul is saying here that in order to inherit the Promise you will need to live a life of active faith. Faith worketh by love (Gal.5: 6); love covers a multitude of sins; therefore **faith is active**. You can always tell the intensity of love by the purposeful preferred activity. They that follow faith and love, desire to live a long healthy life in

Christ and so they are determined to be patient as they do what they believe it takes to achieve the promise.

You cannot profess to have faith without faithfully being involved in something that requires some activity, for faith without works is dead seeing that it stands alone. Faith demands action. Faith always needs a "partner". If you are a preacher then you must preach, teacher then teach, prophet then prophesy, deacon then serve. If you are a storyteller then tell stories because there is a vast audience waiting to hear what God has purposed for you to say. It is for you to find out was is the ordained outlet for your faith to have justification. **Slothfulness in your spiritual assignment leads to the abortion of your faith which is** just as if a pregnant mother goes into an abortion clinic and aborts a child. The child therefore has no future just the ghost of lingering memories of what could have been. Hence, the enemy's job is to abort the seed of faith that has been planted in your life by the word of God, which ender the maturing of your faith.

In Hebrews 11:2, the writer tells us that those who belonged to the Hall of Faith obtained a good report. Not only the ones who are mentioned by name like Abraham,

Able, Enoch, Noah but the **unknown soldiers** in the army of God. All these held strong in faith that they might obtain a better resurrection.

The writer goes on to say, ***"And others had trials of cruel mockings and scourgings, yea, moreover of bonds and imprisonment: They were stoned, they were sawn asunder, were tempted, were slain with the sword: they wandered around in sheepskins and goatskins; being destitute, afflicted, tormented; of whom the world was not worthy:) they wandered in deserts, and in mountains, and in dens and caves of the earth"***. Hebrews 11:36 - 38

You cannot get a report unless you have been actively working at a project. Abraham loved God; he actively became involved more than anyone during his years and was called the father of faith. God loved faithful Abraham and faithful Abraham loved God. When God tested him with his only son, he never doubted that God was able to raise his son Isaac from the dead, which he did in a symbol. There is no place in the life of Abraham which would lead us to imply that he gave up on the promise and was on his way back to Haran. But as Abraham's test got harder his faith got stronger until finally he obtained his son. I would like to tell you that the testing ceased after he had obtained the promise, not so, but his knowledge of God had increased so did his knowledge of the enemy.

Principle: **Your provision will come as a result of the test that you have faithfully endured, which is connected to the vision of God for your life.**

Too many of us are waiting for our provision yet when God shows us His vision we tell him not so God for my vision is over here, this is what I see myself doing. But what would happen if Elijah had not made his way to the widow in Zarephath because he did not see how going to Zarephath complimented his personal vision? This is partly because we recognize that wherever there is a vision there must of necessity be a test. And obedience to the test brings about the unfolding of the vision. But most often we are spoiled disobedient servants who wants our own way.

So God says, since your desire is opposite to mine and I cannot hold you against your will, "suite yourself". But he is hoping that the constant reminder that He has set before you, namely "a blessing and a curse", that you would choose the blessing and live.

And the inference here is not just to live but also to live a life pleasing unto God for which you will be completely provided and that you will in effect leave everyone a little better than you found them.

Principle: Failure to know and choose, that which is right, will always result in suffering wrong.

When God tells you to "suite yourself" that's just what it means because you cannot be dressed in God's armor and your own "suite", which is the condition of many of God's children. Hence there is no provision for those who deter from following after God because provision follows God's vision and lusting after what God has not ordained, will bring great disparity and the corruption of your faithfulness, as you seek to walk the walk of faith

The other virtue that Paul mentions is **patience,** which is endurance, staying power, tolerance, lack of complaint, and persistence. This patience is relative to the endurance of Isaac, as seen in Genesis 26 at the town of **Ezek** and **Sitnah**. Here Isaac endured trials which tested his faith among the neighboring people of Canaan.

Too many of us call for time-out during the trial of our faith only to become slothful. We declare that the extreme nature of our test had not been given full explanation and that were not told about these "unnecessary" trials. It doesn't bother us a bit to train all day and sit around getting fat on knowledge. We don't mind playing war games with silly putty bullets but as soon as the real stuff begins to hit the fan, as soon as we are faced with the real enemy and we see his grenade launchers and hear talk about heavy artillery on the way, it is then that we begin to try to find a way out of the war.

Own Agenda

The problem with 21 century Christian is that too often they joined up for **"frills"**. They have their own agendas, which they believe can be better benefited, by having,

   a) A religious summation of titles on their portfolio

b) The dangling cross around their neck
c) The gold plated names on their bibles
d) Always dressed for success but cannot buy a cripple Crab a crutch.
e) Talking immensely but saying nada

But permit me to draw a parallel between a **soldier after the flesh** who serves in the military and a **spiritual soldier** who is fashioned for the army of the Lord. For suddenly, its wartime and now you are dressed in fatigues with sixty-two pounds of ammunition and personal items. Your training has suddenly become a reality. You are in the midst of war and you will only have dependency on the things that prepared you for this moment.

Now, while you are on the battlefield, instead of a shower or a bath, your bath comes in a small paper towel, which carries the odor of janitor in a drum. Then to add it all off, you are given a shovel and told, "for your potty".

Now the real fighter in times of war doesn't look for a **"way out"** but he looks for a **"way in"** to the battle because he wants to make an impact on the enemy's defenses.

Likewise, the spiritual soldier realizes that the Lord, upon whom he depends, has now become his strength and his fortress as he utilizes the whole armor of God. He solidly trusts in the Lord, for the Lord is his strength. Psalms 91 takes a new meaning for him. He sees the Lord as his deliverer from the snare of the fowler, and from the noisome pestilence. He knows that he will overcome and so he gives no place for doubt. **He knows that he his Lord's warrior and not satan's punk**.

A real soldier in the army of the Lord says how can I use what I have learned to make a difference? He doesn't sit around and procrastinate, or reason away the right approach that he may have the victory over his enemy, neither is he slothful.

He knows that he has been given skill-set to make a difference. And no matter what skill-set or arm of the military force he has been given, whether marine, a grunt, a sniper, a paratrooper, coastguard, engineer or a Navy seal, the topmost of his intention is national defense on which there can be placed no monetary value. He proudly sing the song and make it his anthem,

"Onward, Christian soldier, marching on to war,
With the cross of Jesus going on before,
Christ, the royal master, leads against the foe;
Forward into battle see his banners go".

Some soldiers however, have become "hired hands" or mercenaries but in God's army there are no mercenaries. Mercenaries kill for payment and will go to the highest bidder but the saint of the Lord Jesus Christ knows no other loyalty but God.

Again, there are some who goes by the name of "soldier" but are not for when the fighting begins they seek to cover themselves. They are the fake that says, **"please let another go and I'll watch and see as he makes the difference".**
Jesus speaks about attitude similar to theirs in the Gospel of John. He says,

But he that is a hireling, and not a shepherd, whose own the sheep are not, seeth the wolf coming, and leaveth the sheep, and fleeth; and the wolf catcheth them, and scattereth them.

The hireling fleeth, because he is a hireling, and careth not for the sheep." Jn.10:12

Soldier having such an attitude of a hireling is nothing but slothfulness on display.

A real soldier says, "This is my country, the cities and the rivers, the mountains are mine too, and they belong to me as a citizen. Therefore, will I protect it from all enemies!

I'll never forget **George C Scott in the movie, "Patton"** as he visited an army hospital. While greeting the wounded, there was one soldier who showed no outward signs of suffering. When the General learned of his reason for being there he became furious and sent the fake back to his post.

Principle: Sometimes, in war, the coward and the enemy are best placed in the same trench for either of them is in good standing.

Sworn Promise

The writer of Hebrews refers to **a promise** and **an oath** that God made to Abraham because of his faithfulness and the Book of Genesis give testimony. The scripture reads, *"And said, By myself have I sworn, saith the LORD, for because thou hast done this thing, and hast not withheld thy son, thine only son:*
17 That in blessing I will bless thee, and in multiplying I will multiply thy seed as the stars of the heaven, and as the sand which is upon the sea shore; and thy seed shall possess the gate of his enemies;" Genesis 22:16-17

God was pleased with the faith of Abraham who did not stumble at the promises but believed him for Isaac. The word "Isaac" means laughter and when you remain faithful as Abraham, God swore that he would bless and bring "laughter" into your life.

Did God bless Abraham? Yes, he blessed him immensely with laughter! And even though it took 25 years for his son to manifest, it was worth the wait.

Some of you God as planted a seed in your spirit but instead of being as Abraham, you are running the risk of allowing the spirit of slothfulness rob you of your seed. Therefore, God is sending me to echo His word, and that is, you should not abort your seed! Wait for it! It shall manifest and it shall bring you "laughter".

A Place of Disadvantage

Slothfulness is not a privilege nor an advantage in the kingdom of God but a **place of disadvantage** where those who have fainted; where the lonely, the ones who have been provoked unto unrighteousness, the ones who have become dysfunctional, the ones who have given up on being victors in the trials of faith and patience, who have now **doubted the promise** and the **oath of God,** when He swore by himself, for there was none greater by which to swear, that in blessing He would bless and in multiplying He would multiply.

Further Identification of the spirit of Slothfulness

Let us look at some other scriptures that will give us added understanding of the curse of slothfulness.

"The *hand of the diligent shall bear rule: but the slothful shall be under tribute*". Proverbs 12:24

In this case, slothful comes from the Hebrew word "**remiyah**" pronounced *rem-ee-yaw'* and means; *remissness*, **treachery***:* —**deceit** (-ful, -fully), false, guile, idle, slack.

This is saying that a slothful person is one of deceit; he is one that **bears false witness**, that's filled with guile and hypocrisy. Here is a person that is trying to live a privileged life but because of his deceitfulness, because he wants to acquire his gains falsely, he will continually fail at life until he learns that **righteousness must be a way of life**.

The other meaning of **slothful** is the word **remissness** from the word, "remiss" which means, to be careless, negligent, **lax**, **inattentive**, and to be **inconsistent**.

In Proverb 12:27 the scripture says,

"**The *slothful (remiyah)* man roasteth not that which he took in hunting: but the substance of a diligent man is precious.**"

The slothful man is one who,
a) Fail to realize the advantages of God's divine plan for him
b) He takes no comfort in what God has provided
c) He is plagued by apprehensiveness, always concerned by his own unfettered emotions.

Let us pray

Father, we ask you to open the eyes of our understanding. Help us to know your direction that we may be pleasing unto you daily. We pray that the choices we make will continually glorify your holy name.

We bind up every spirit of slothfulness that has been sent to attack me and cast it out in Jesus name.

We pray that the council of the Lord concerning my life will be established and that the word of God may have free course in my life.

In Jesus Name

CHAPTER 4

The Way of a Slothful Man Is As a Hedge of Thorns

Thorns can be beneficial depending on its use. In fact thorny hedges were used to prevent certain animals from getting into areas that were either used for gardening or as a fence around living quarters. In the Bible an "hedge" is mentioned in **Ezekiel 22:30**,

And I sought for a man among them, ***that should make up the hedge****, and stand in the gap before me for the land, that I should not destroy it: but I found none.*

This implies that there was a **grievous breach** in the moral state and the attitude of the people. No one was found with the "right mix" to stand in the gap; to faithfully exhort, reprove and intercede for the people. Slothfulness was over the land.

It is a **shameful indictment** when the God of all the earth looks over an entire nation and gives such a summation that none was found who had the love for his people or for God. There was none that would be willing to **disavow their personal idolatry for the good of the nation**. And not only for the good of the nation but of our individual welfare because a nation is a group of individuals who identify with a purpose or aim in consideration of a continued existence.

But the attitude of the people is that they were so blinded in their worldly craft that they didn't give a care whether they lived or died. They were only living for the gusto of today and not the existence in tomorrow.

Modern society has fallen into the same trap and the system that the devil used yesterday, he found out that it still work and so he his making a profit from destroying man's soul. It is as if he is urinating on our head and turns around and tells us that it is rainfall. After all, that has been working so wonderful for him that he is thinking, why change it if it works?

Let's us look again at Ezekiel 22:30 which says,
And I sought for a man among them, **that should make up the hedge***, and stand in the gap before me for the land, that I should not destroy it: but I found none.*

In these days God is always in search of a man or woman to make a stand for His people. And with as many persons as the earth is populated, likewise is the call of God that not a single one should perish. The favorite verse among evangelist is John 3:16, Jesus speaking said,
"For God so love the world, that He gave His only begotten Son, that whomsoever believeth in him should not perish, but have everlasting life."

Therefore, there is no need for us to worry about what God has called us to do, for it is given that the job of every believer is to pray for those who have not yet believed. That is profound statement because most believers are sitting around waiting on their gifts while the people that they are called to reach are running around like little children left alone in a satanic nursery called, "the world". We that are saved are to be watchmen for the souls of them who are in the world and have yet to develop a relationship with the Most High.

God is depending on us for we are his hands and his feet upon the earth. We are God's mouthpieces to create opportunities for the unsaved, the disenfranchised, the oppressed and all them that are afflicted.

Therefore the Lord would say, "**Is there not a cause?** Should we that have been given salvation merely sit in church for one hour on Sundays while the rest of the world is speedily going to hell. Should we not be accountable for something other than getting our emotions stroked for one hour out of a week of hours and feel justified that we have fulfilled our God given purpose.

Can you create a comfortable spiritual lifestyle out of one hour in seven days? What wife would have a reasonable amount of intimacy from her spouse if she only saw him one hour per week when she knew he was able to give much more?

We better beware, for God has been merciful to us even though we have committed spiritual adultery. But how long will the mercy last before He signs for our spiritual divorcement? How long shall the adultery last before God says that this marriage is going nowhere!
Is there not a cause that we should make up a hedge around our families, our communities, the blocks in which we live and our cities?

Is there not a cause to take the city? For each member of the body of Christ must take the city in which they live, in other words they must build up the wall of intercession around the city.

Principle: Unless the wall around the city is built up then every "beast" will have its part in reigning over the city.

There can be no effective rule without a "wall" or a "hedge". **There can be no effective rule without boundaries ".** To take the city is to build up its walls. So you must take the city or take hold of the city, build up its walls by prayer and intercession so the satanic principalities cannot prevail over the lives of the people. A leader, who is tolerant of the will of the people instead of the will of God for the people, will soon lose their appointment as king Saul lost his appointment. God had set up a boundary for Saul and Saul went beyond that boundary and God called it, "witchcraft".

It has been proven that when prayer ceases the "beast" will take over the land because there is no hedge, no protection, no possibility of evasion from the enemy's assault, no fortification, and your shield will become ineffective and you will have no confidence in your armor. To have no confidence in your armor is to have no confidence in the God who is your armor for every military armament that you have been given belongs to God and so our weaknesses are because of us and not God's armor.

God's armor was given to you complete and will remain in the shape it was given. Your armor never gets old, it always remain new. Our shield doesn't get holes from battle use because our shields cannot be penetrated nor can the sword we have been given break or becomes dull but will always remain sharp and consistent, dutifully performing every action with precision.

Hence, with the hedge there is security, safety and shelter and the individual families are strengthened and revived. Therefore, the breakdown of families will become non-existent and righteousness will prevail.
But the spirit of slothfulness seeks out a breach in the city wall and influences the people of the city into immorality and sin.

Allow me to share with you from a quote of **E. Stanly Jones**, as he tells us about the seven deadly sins he has had occasion to experience. He says,

" Seven deadly sins: politics without principle, wealth without work, pleasure without conscience, knowledge without character, business without morality, science without humanity, and worship without sacrifice."

Unfortunately this is indeed the state of our society today and that is why each individual believer must come to a **point of inner or personal revival** that is preceded by soul cleansing that the Spirit of the Lord might move upon the land to restore our broken down walls. After the walls are "built up", then there is safety and industry will prosper within the "gap" that is established in the city. The "gap" will then be able to entertain **the promises** of the Lord and God's righteousness shall bear rule.

So now the Lord would ask the believers who have been given legal authority to create "gap" by the words out of their mouth, he would say, "where now is the "gap" that you have made for me so that I can bless those whom I have called you to reach?
Therefore, one thing that the favored sons and daughters of God cannot do   is to become complacent because of the influence of the spirit of slothfulness.

In Proverbs 15:19, says,
"The way of the slothful (atsel) man is as a hedge of thorns".

The manner of life by which the slothful man has chosen to go, hides him from his true purpose. There is no **revelation** in this way but only that which he has surmised in his own selfish heart since he has chosen not to identify with the principled information of the true God. Therefore his way is difficult because the **divine language**, which he should be using to quicken his mortal body and bring prosperity to his soul, he now uses in reverse because of the pessimistic influence of the spirit of slothfulness.

The Hebrew word used here for describing the man with a slothful spirit is **"astel"** and so rather than being the one who builds a hedge, his indolent behavior confines him to a mediocre life instead of a spirit filled life in Christ Jesus. He is described, as having an indolent and sluggard attitude therefore his way becomes a "hedge of thorns".

The word indolent means laid-back, lethargic, sluggish, and idle.
- His un-renewed mind **imagines ten thousand difficulties in the way** which cannot be surmounted

- **All are the creations of his own imagination**, and that imagination is formed by his slothfulness

Slothful Spies

Israel was pitch in the wilderness of Paran from which place Moses sent out sent out spies into the land to search it out. These men had been taken one from each tribe and one that was notable among the people. They went and searched out the land saw that it was a good land but yet everyone brought back an evil report all but two, Caleb and Joshua. The report they brought was written in Numbers 13:30 - 33.

"And Caleb stilled the people before Moses, and said, Let us go up at once, and possess it; for we are well able to overcome it.
^{31} But the men that went up with him said, We be not able to go up against the people; for they are stronger than we.
^{32} And they brought up an evil report of the land which they had searched unto the children of Israel, saying, The land, through which we have gone to search it, is a land

that eateth up the inhabitants thereof; and all the people that we saw in it are men of a great stature.

"And there we saw the giants, the sons of Anak, which come of the giants: and we were in our own sight as grasshoppers, and so we were in their sigh."

The ten spies of Israel imagined themselves as **grasshoppers** and they made a **declaration,** which was, that was exactly the way the sons of Anak saw them.

Principle: You are always declaring your belief and you grow into what you declare.

Remember, you are what you believe that you are and God is a God of faith and cannot legally move you further than your belief. Therefore, the children of Israel who did not believe that God could do as he had promised became complacent and died a defeated people in the desert. Therefore, this was what the holy God said to those that could not believe,

Numbers 14:20-24,

"And the LORD said, I have pardoned according to thy word:

²¹ But as truly as I live, all the earth shall be filled with the glory of the LORD.

²² Because all those men which have seen my glory, and my miracles, which I did in Egypt and in the wilderness, and have tempted me now these ten times, and have not hearkened to my voice;

²³ Surely they shall not see the land which I sware unto their fathers, neither shall any of them that provoked me see it:

²⁴ But my servant Caleb, because he had another spirit with him, and hath followed me fully, him will I bring into the land whereunto he went; and his seed shall possess it".

The Lord promised that you would possess what belongs to him if you by faith and patience endure and believe his word.

Chapter Five

A Slothful Man Neglect His Work

He also that is slothful— Proverbs 18:9 says, ***"A slothful man neglects his work, and the materials go to ruin: the "brother", he destroys the materials."***

In this case it comes from the word **raphah,** *raw-faw'* A primitive root**; to** *slacken* (in many applications, literally or figuratively): -abate, cease, consume, draw [toward evening], fail, (be) faint, be (wax) feeble, forsake, idle, leave, let alone (go, down), (be) slack, stay, be still, be slothful, (be) weak (-en).

Some of us are thinking about **slackening our hands** from what the Lord has called us to do. Maybe because of

provocation, distress or distractions of the world system but God says, "Don't be slothful, is it not the time of harvesting, is it not time for the collection of your rewards!

The Lord would say, don't let the opposition of the enemy be a consideration! The Lord would say that, I would be your defense, look not to the right or the left, but remain focus on that thing which I the Lord have commanded thee.

David in 1Samuel 11:1-2 had become **slack** and the spirit of slothfulness directed him towards **Bathsheba.**
As been pointed out in chapter eleven 2nd Samuels, it was a time when Kings go out to war; when the spiritual sons of God, the **vanguards** in the army of the Lord, the **gatekeepers**, the **intercessors**, the ones that stand in the gap; the ones whom God uses to birth things into the earth realm; the kings of the most high God; they were called into spiritual warfare.

It was the **season of rearrangement**; of taking down principalities and jurisdictional spirits; in short, it was a call to prayer, but as David was found slack in the day of his temptation so are the typical "David" today.

God wanted David to conceive and give birth to new lands and new ideas, new territories, to expand the kingdom to the glory of God but instead of doing true service to God, he was doing service to the flesh and sowing seeds in the womb of Bathsheba. When you sow to the flesh the end result is death.

Notice that the failure was not in Bathsheba but failure, as slackness, was in the **heart of David**. In other words, David was the one who failed; Bathsheba was merely the element that he used to support his act.

Slothfulness is directional and as a policeman directs traffic so is slothfulness trying to direct the saints of God in an effort to minimize the effect of their calling in God. **Slothfulness is a spirit of distraction born in confusion**.

Never as there been a time when the saints of God are in need of the **direction of the Holy Ghost** as they do now because of the supernatural opposition of the enemy,

The enemy, recognizing this need in God's people for the Holy Spirit's direction is on alert for those without the spirit of discernment, those who are weak, that he may bring them into weariness in the hope of them cursing God. He is effective against those whose minds are undisciplined for they refuse to pray until their situation changes. He is sending those **possessing the spirit of divination among them, to distract them and abort their purposes.**

This spirit otherwise called python is preying upon those that are undiscerning giving them false directions to get the saints to slacken the hold on the promise and the oath of God.

Paul warns in 2 Timothy 3:1-3 (KJV) that,

¹ This know also, that in the last days perilous times shall come. ² For men shall be lovers of their own selves, covetous, boasters, proud, blasphemers, disobedient to parents, unthankful, unholy, ³ Without natural affection, trucebreakers, false accusers, incontinent, fierce, despisers of those that are good,

Traitors, heady, high-minded, lovers of pleasures more than lovers of God;
⁵ Having a form of godliness, but denying the power thereof: from such turn away.

Yet another Proverbs 19:24 says, *"A slothful man hideth his hand in his bosom"*. Slothful here is from the Hebrew word *"astel"* and gives the definition to such a person,

a) He is too lazy to feed himself
b) He lacks confidence in the power of the word
c) He may have tried it but upon opposition he withdrew.
d) It is like dipping his hands once in the dish, but he is too lazy to put it in a second time.
e) Because of his excessive slothfulness, he would rather starve than put himself to the trouble to eat, so he refuses to feed himself.
f) He is oppressed

This man, who has **lost his confidence** and ended up being a spiritual sloth, will pretend that the weather conditions are unfavorable and so he will let the proper time of seed sowing elapse so that he may have an excuse for not cultivating the land.

Sowing in the Right Season – God has given his people the Spirit of discernment to not only discerned spirits but also discerning the times and seasons. The Lord God has given us an anointing even far greater than that of the **sons of Issachar**.

The Bible says of Issachar, that he is a strong ass couching between two burdens or "couching between the hurdles" likely the pens or stalls in which the cattle were lodged. But it also goes on to say that they were bearer of burdens and payer of tribute rather than undertake the struggle for independence and liberty.

However Adam Clarke Commentary on the Old Testament said according to the Targum claims that they were all astronomers and astrologers. The sons of Issachar "**were skilled in fixing the beginnings of years, the commencement of months, and the intercalation of months and years; skillful in the changes of the moon, and the fixing of the lunar solemnities to their proper times; skillful also in the doctrine of the solar periods; astrologers in signs and stars, that they might show Israel what to do**".

Regardless of the posture of the sons of Issachar, we as born-again believers have to sow in the right season and as spiritual farmer, **we must so when the anointing is right!** In the natural, seeds aren't sown in the winter season; the snow on the ground and the low temperatures makes it inadvisable to farm. In the same way, there is a spiritual season to sow and to expect a bountiful harvest.

But the man who has lost his confidence refuse to sow in any season and ends up being a sloth.
For when it is time to sow, the word, money, love and some times his manual labor he will bury his head in the sand of opposition, which may come as discouragement, or some agent of dysfunction.

These are merely excuses he stands behind to hide his sloth for God has already promised and swore by Himself that He would be his prosperity.

Proverbs 21:25 adds that, *"The desire of the slothful (astel) killeth him; for his hands refuse to labor"*.

The man desires to eat, drink, and be clothed: but because he does not labor, in the end he dies with this desire in his heart. He nevertheless refuses to venture into the unknown and in the end he envies those who possess plenty through their endeavor.

Hence in verse 26, he is said to covet greedily all the day long, while the righteous, who have been committed to industry, has enough to eat, and some to spare.

Here we have another instance in Proverbs 22:13, where, **"The slothful man saith, There is a lion without"**.

After deliverance from the spirit slothfulness, then these imaginary difficulties and dangers will be no more. But because he thinks there is a lion in the way, he will not go out into the town for food, employment or even to develop his social structure.

Let us pray

Lord we come against the spirit of spiritual slumber in the lives of the people in our assemblies.

We stand on God's word and declare that the spirit of slothfulness, slumber and laxity is under our feet.

Thank you Lord that you have given us power over all the power of the enemy and nothing shall by any means harm us.

Thank you that the Spirit of Life in Christ Jesus has made me free from the law of sin and death.

Therefore we take authority over every spirit of bondage and command the enemy never to return to our homes.

We declare that every one that calls upon the name of the Lord shall be delivered.

We receive our deliverance now, in Jesus Name

Chapter Six

Breaking Free to Spiritual Empowerment

The saints of the Most High God must become aware that **empowerment and deliverance from a slothful spirit is available in order that you might create a new identity** but this will only come as you walk in **obedience to God's word.** This entails certain requirements,

a.   **The right location** – mental/soul, spiritual place; that mean being in a place of Joy, a place of Peace (not a place of fear and contention)

b.   **The right season** – don't complain but proclaim (1:28); confess that your season has come - Most often we **create our own season by our words**

c. **The right relationship** – You must be within the right fellowship, communion, etc. The people in your proximity must be people of faith who are striving to be in alignment with the Spirit of God and not the world. Do not become condemned because you are unacquainted with the first base super star of the Yankees. Give glory and honor to God that he uses you for a far more important detail. For when they have an emergency prayer request, they will not seek out football or baseball but they will seek you because of your relationship with God. They will seek you out because they know that God has empowered you for His glory.

In Colossians 1:29 the Apostle Paul speaks of **empowerment**, he wrote,
"Whereunto I also labour, striving according to his working, which worketh in me mightily."

Amplified says,
For this I labor [unto weariness], striving with all the superhuman energy, which he so mightily enkindles and works within me.

Paul says, "**I also Labor**", meaning that,

a.   He was under the employment of God whose faithfulness was unquestioned, Rom. 1:1

b.   He has faith in his employer – that his employer will produce the evidence of his workings in him

c.   He is a part of a divine net work- a body fitted together proclaiming the power of God unto salvation (Rom. 1:16)

d.   He labor with the utmost zeal and earnestness

e.   Striving according to his working, meaning the strength with which God has most powerfully furnished in us, the spiritual empowerment over all the power of the enemy.

We know that changing one's spiritual identity from one who has allowed himself to be fashioned after the spirit of slothfulness to come into his true birthright as a child of God is not a temporary occurrence but a daily walk. It is not stationery working but as soon as God as taken you to a place of maturity then he will say, "Get up, you have miles to go and things to learn".

What I am saying is that, God is not empowering you to be comfortable but to always strive to be better in Him. Therefore, for a Christian there is no place called, "**Recline in the world**" but there is always a place called "**Recline in the Word**" (Rest in the word). Recline in the world for a Christian is an illegal place.

For example, while the children of Israel were in Babylonian captivity they were expected to carry on and increase in their relationship with God even though they were in bonds. God had given them a chance to prove their love and honor for him and for each other. This stripping was God's way of restoration without their "interruptions". You see the Lord does his best work uninterrupted. When he made the world he did it without the interruption of man and with this he had notable comment that it was good. But soon man came and woman out of man and their desire was to do what seem right to them and not to God. In other words, God wants to get you to a place in which you are looking up and not down and around.
Israel had become wrapped up in **service to man**, idols and every other thing but God. Therefore God called for a

realignment that could only be done with their eyes fixed on the one who had made man and given man dominion over the earth.

Therefore he brought them back to that **point of connection** where they knew that the communal activity among them and with their God tended to success and they remembered that reclining in the World was always the reason for their captivity.

God always provided a **vanguard**, which showed the people that though they were in captivity to Babylon yet their God was not a captive. And so the Lord would keep His sons like Daniel, Hananiah, Mishael and Azariah empowered before them as a **light for the nation** to spearhead in the service of the Lord within the kings court.

The Spiritual Empowerment or the Workings of God includes such workings to benefit the believer in bringing destruction to the spirit of slothfulness. Jesus said, *"Behold I give unto you power (exousia) to tread on serpents and scorpions, and over all the power (dunamis) of the enemy; and nothing shall by any means hurt you.*

We have to know that God has down loaded certain benefits unto us and there is no way that the enemy can attain victory. Let us look at the word "**power**" in the Greek language as used in this passage from Luke 10:19,

- **Exousia**

1. Power of choice, liberty of doing as one pleases, noting that the ordinances contained in the Book of Moses has been blotted out Col.2: 14
2. The ability or strength with which one is endued, which he either possesses or exercises

- **Dunamis** - strength power, ability

The inherent power, **power residing in a thing by virtue of its nature**, or which a person or thing exerts and puts forth

b) Power for performing miracles
c) Moral power and excellence of soul
d) The power and influence, which belong to riches and wealth
e) Power and resources arising from numbers

(Taken from Strong's Dictionary)

Therefore, we see that by the power of God believers no longer has to be under the condemnation of their old nature. The Holy Spirit as changed that old nature and given us a new nature that answers to the Head of the Church, the Lord Jesus. With this in mind, the spirit of slothfulness is bound up and loosed to where God would have them to go. And so, whatever is the nature of the glorified Son; this is now become our new nature upon receiving the resurrected Christ to be our Lord and savior by faith.

The spirit of slothfulness belonged to our old nature and some of us are clinging to portions of our old nature because we haven't recognized that we are a new creature in Christ Jesus. We are now become a kingdom of priest and kings. Some believers, because of a lack of understanding, resist leaving some things behind, old friends, and old games and this is a deterrent to their spiritual success. But we must confess that we are new creatures in Christ and that the forces of lingering lust and pride cannot prevail against us. We must declare that we are not short on insight but is strong in the Lord to whom we can say, "Great is his faithfulness!

The power of God will keep you even when you cannot keep yourself (1Pet.1: 5). In fact, that is exactly what it was meant to do because the more dependent we are on God, the more successful we become. God is always faithful and he has already made payment for the consequences of our sin. God's mercy will always endure and your faith in him will be a shield until the revelation dawn upon you that you are more than a conqueror. Recognizing your newness in Christ Jesus is to step off into the area where nothing is impossible with God.

God wants you to know that you have been graced for a divine purpose. You have been fashioned and customized for the workings of God. The Lord would have us to know that we have been detailed by the application of the threefold witness mentioned 1Jn.5: 7, 8

a. Holy Ghost - Jn.16: 26
b. Word
c. Blood

Great Conflict

Howbeit, sometimes we are in great conflict because of the spirit of slothfulness and so let me piggyback on the scripture in Colossians 2:1 where Paul says,

For I would that ye knew what **great conflict** *I have for you, and for them at Laodicea, and for as many as have not seen my face in the flesh.*

Principle: Great conflict requires great suffering but the power of God will bring you out.

Even though you have a **changed nature you will still be in conflict**. As long as you remain on the earth you will be in conflict. Only the dead are free of conflict.

But because we have been spiritually empowered, the working of the grace of God will encourage our hearts by uniting us in love for one another and for the Lord Jesus.

The goal of spiritual empowerment is that,
   I. You might be delivered from the darkness of this world which include spiritual slothfulness
   II. You may know the mystery of God. This is done as we go through the hidden treasures of wisdom and knowledge found in the revelation of God's word.

The result of spiritual empowerment is to be:

a.   Rooted and grounded in him

b.   Strengthened in faith

c.   Filled with thanksgiving

d.   Prosperous as your soul prosper

Principle: You cannot have conflict without opposition.

In short, spiritual empowerment is therefore, to know the mystery of God and be obedient to what has been revealed. Hence, because of this revelation, our prayer should be Lord, teach me your ways that I may overcome today's conflict. The word of the Lord tells us that "before honor is humility" but the Lord will deliver you from all persecution.

My friend, remember that tomorrow will bring the same conflicts unless you have overcome them today. Therefore you alone are responsible for what God has revealed to you, now take authority and dispossess the spirit of slothfulness.

So God says, **"Command ye me"**, that means **take command of my word** so that it will prevail over today's conflicts.

Therefore, do not be afraid of conflict – It takes effort; **agonizing**, agony to appropriate anything that is of value. The Apostle Paul compared conflict to a contest; a wrestling match; severe struggling with pain and suffering.

- **Remember that anguish is the reflection on evil that is already past, while agony is a struggle with evil at the time present.**

The word **agony** is only used in the New Testament by Luke (Luke 22:44) to describe our Lord's struggle in Gethsemane.

CHAPTER SEVEN

Attainment of Victory

In this chapter we will deal with overcoming the spirit of slothfulness. We have been over several scriptures in the previous chapters and as Solomon said in his book of Ecclesiastes, "This is the conclusion of the whole matter: Fear God and keep his commandments: for this is the whole duty of man".

If fearing God and keeping his commandments is the road to success in God then it is also the pathway to victory over the spirit of slothfulness. So we will begin with the first of the master commandment.

1. **We overcome the spirit of slothfulness by development of Love:**

Apostle Paul commands us that in the midst of conflict we are to love one another. Love is the element that fosters **spiritual empowerment** that results in,

a. Power

b. Blessing

Power and blessing is needed to overcome the spirit of slothfulness.

It was Erich Fromm who said that infantile love follows a principle: **"I love because I am loved." Immature love says: "I love you because I need you." Mature love says: "I need you because I love you."**

Love supplies the power to overcome the darkness of this world, "for God so love that he gave His only Son."

- **People that are oppressed by the spirit of slothfulness must be made to feel that they are needed**.

That stirs up hope on which faith can be built to break the bondage and bring them back into living a sound spiritual life. To pull away from one on whom the enemy has been waging full scale attack is to commit fratricide and we become no better than abortionist for we are denying that soul a chance to pursue his God given agenda.

"No single factor has so limited the Christian church down through the years as man's inhumanity to man—sometimes outright cruelty, but far more often, sheer lovelessness." George Sweeting
"People don't go where the action is they go where the love is." Jess Moody

2. **We overcome the spirit of slothfulness by:**
Application of the Blood of Jesus
We have to remember that before the crucifixion the sin memory of each born again believer was merely covered therefore the memory still remained.   But once the crucifixion was over and Jesus Christ ascended to the throne of God with the blood of sprinkling, the word says, *"And their sins and iniquities will I remember no more."* Hebrew 10:17
Why? For this is the result of a new covenant built upon better promise
It says also in Jeremiah 31:34,

"*And they shall teach no more every man his neighbour, and every man his brother, saying, Know the LORD: for they shall all know me, from the least of them unto the greatest of them, saith the LORD: **for I will forgive their iniquity, and I will remember their sin no more***".

Now the earthly temple is patterned after the heavenly, which follows the acts of propitiation in which blood had to be sprinkled on the mercy seat to atone for the sin of the people.

It says in Hebrews 9:23,

"***That the pattern of things in the heavens should be purified with these; but the heavenly things themselves with better sacrifices than these***".

After the resurrection, the Lord Jesus had to complete his priestly duties in heaven before he sat down. This implies that according to the pattern given to Moses, he also as a **high priest** had to sprinkle his blood over the heavenly utensils within the heavenly temple.

Therefore we can recognize why it was that when Mary was first to the tomb early on the first day of the week or Resurrection Day and saw the Lord Jesus whom she believed to have been the gardener, on recognizing the Lord, He told her, **"*Do not touch me, for I have not yet ascended unto the Father*"**.

He had not yet presented himself unto the Father with the eternal blood sacrifice so that the pattern, which He had shown Moses in the mount, could be once and for all completed. If he had been touch by corruptible flesh then the blood sacrifice would have been in vain for it could not achieve it's purpose in the heavenly temple. He had not yet appeared unto God.

The book of Hebrews clearly states, speaking of Jesus Christ, by his own **blood** he entered once into the holy place, having obtained eternal redemption for us. The Lord Jesus is now seated at the right hand of the Father in Heaven and you now have permission to **plead his blood** against every **slothful sin** that tries to come into your presence. You have been given the keys of the kingdom that "whatsoever ye shall bind on earth shall be bound in heaven; and whatsoever you shall loose on earth shall be loosed in heavens.

3. **We overcome by showing compassion that the victim is encouraged to change.**

There is an aged old story of a monk who met a beggar on a country roadside while on his journey to a far away land. This beggar, beholding the approaching Monk, held out his cup expecting mercy from the minister of the cloth. The monk saw this as an opportunity to do good service and so he reached down into his pockets expecting to have some pocket change but found no money. The beggar looked at him with dismay as if to say, please, can you check again?

In these days you cannot go by a beggar without having some alms in your possession because he will pass judgement and exclaim how dare you walk on God's green earth with no money in your pocket? How dare you be penniless and come into my presence? The beggars are asserting their roles as beggars and so they are expecting the sons of God to walk in the divine prosperity that has been given them and so they are expecting to receive something that will bring about an atmospheric change for good after the sons of God has been in their presence. For as Peter came upon the beggar that was set at the temple gate and brought change so must we bring change in the places where God has set us.

We can declare to them that God loves them and that you are decreeing a masterful improvement in your life that will take them from struggle into financial and spiritual abundance. As sons of God you have the ability to make decrees, you have the authority to plant word seed from which God is obligated to improve or remove.

In our story of the monk and the beggar had absolutely no currency but he remembered the precious stone that he had tied into his waist. It was all that he had of value. It was the sum total of all that he possessed. That was akin to him parting with his last meal.

Sometimes God will bring a circumstance that is only a test because he desires to show you the **condition of your heart**. Let me make sure you understand that God doesn't need to know the condition of your heart because he already knows it but he wants to make sure that you recognize the condition and why God was unable to give you some of the things you have been requesting.

You see the condition of the heart is the reception site for God's payload.

The writer of Proverbs 4:23 declares,
"Keep thy heart with all diligence; for out of it are the issues of life"
God's word says, above every charge keep your heart because life issueth out of it. It is the heart that makes or breaks an individual or ministry.

Your heart is like a landing strip, planes outgoing /incoming but if the landing strip is in serious disrepair then no aircraft can land. Your loaded aircraft are out there and they see the need to land because they know that you have a need but they cannot land and must pass over and find the next airfield that is available. That why someone is driving your new car, sailing your boat and living in your new house that initially had your name on them. Fix your heart and watch your "planes" begin to land.

In our story, after some thought the monk came to a resolve that the beggar had a greater need than he did and so he loose the precious stone from the safe keeping around his waist and gave the beggar that was his only possession apart from the cloths he wore. With a relaxed countenance he turned and continued on his journey. I have found that doing what God would have you is the only peaceful solution to any circumstance. Often we hold on to what is in our possession only to regret for the lack of peace and the undue discomfort that follows.

After the monk had traveled a few paces he heard the beggar in the background crying out for more. He was astounded. Finally the beggar arrived at the place were the monk stood and said, "**Give me more**? The monk was bewildered. After all he had given him all he had and this man had the audacity to ask for more!

The beggar said to the surprised monk, "**Give me some of what inspired you to give me your most precious possession!**

Of all the years that he had been asking for alms he had yet to see such an offering of kindness and compassion. It woke up the place in him called "**change**".

The beggar was **inspired** and **encouraged** to change and the monk was encouraged because he had gained a far greater reward. There is no greater miracle than to see a sinner born again and a backslider **restored**.

In Isaiah 58:12 the prophet says, *"And they that shall be of thee shall build the old waste places: thou shalt raise up the foundations of many generations; and thou shalt be called, The **repairer of the breach, The restorer of paths to dwell in**."*

When you encourage someone you not only **repair the breach** that has been weaved into the lives of the victims by the spirit of slothfulness but you are in effect a **restorer of** paths to dwell in for your words goes into the **deep pockets of contention** that cries out for deliverance and closure and you release the very Spirit of Grace who will with power confound the adversary and justify the unrighteous by the blood of the Lamb.

The satanic foundations that the spirit of slothfulness raised up may have been the result of situations and conditions that came upon the victim as a result of a **generational curse** that now **stands between the poor soul and his tomorrow**.

These take the form of,
1. The anger that you are always fighting,
2. The inability to work with other folk; wants to sit by yourself all the way in the corner
3. The resentment you feel towards leader
4. The inability to take correction
5. The sexual sin and perversion that hinders you
6. The **rejection** that combats your soul that shows its effects **inwardly** in the form of,
   a) **Self hatred** and guilt, Gal.3: 13
   b) **Feeling of inadequacy** and inferior, Rom.12: 2 "And be not conformed …"
   c) **Anxiety**, Lk.12: 11, 25, Phil.4: 6, "*Be careful for nothing; but in everything by prayer and supplication let your request be made known unto God*", 1Peter5: 7 "Casting all your **care**".

4. **We overcome by promoting a conflict resolution strategy, that is**,
    I. Having a connection with the Holy Spirit
    II. Be confident in the word that God has given you for your deliverance from the spirit of slothfulness
    III. Make and activate your decision
    IV. Expect the Holy Ghost to work in you mightily

We pray that something was said in these pages that brought you consolation and encouraged your heart that now you may with boldness move from your place of comfort to a place of great faith. And I leave with you this verse from Isaiah 60:1, "Arise, shine; for thy light is come, and the glory of the Lord is risen upon thee".

Thank you for giving me the privilege to take you to God's place of blessing.

Let Us Pray

Lord we thank you for your blessed assurance as we make our daily walk with you.

We thank you for your mercy and grace that worketh in us richly.

We pray that you will fill our heart with pure love for the members of my household and the body of Christ in general.

We declare by your word that the Lord will command His lovingkindness in the daytime, and in the night His song shall be with me.

Thank you that have drawn the souls of men unto you by your lovingkindness.

I declare this day that the Lord, the eternal God, is my refuge and underneath are the everlasting arms.

I thank you for being the God that comforts me and surrounds me with your protection all the daylong.

I bind every spirit of slothfulness that comes at the crossroad of life and I loose them to dry places in the name of Jesus.

I declare that my eyes have been anointed by the Lord to keep me from time wasting decisions.

I declare the anointing of holy joy upon my life as the Holy Spirit sends forth the refreshing of the Lord.

I praise you Father for you have loosed the bonds of wickedness and you have let the oppressed go free to the glory of God.

I reverse the curse of the spirit of slothfulness and sever every illegal plan against my dwelling.

I thank you for the engrafted word of God that is able to save many souls.

I now ask for a spirit of repentance over this nation and ask for an anointing that will save many souls.

I declare that the Lord God is one God, merciful, holy, faithful with lovingkindness that is shed abroad into the hearts of men.

I pray a special anointing on this book to touch every soul for their deliverance, healing, business and ministerial success.

I give glory to God for allowing me to walk out of the realm of failure and into the arena of success.

I thank the Lord that now I am a new creation, redeemed by the blood of Jesus.

I give glory to God for household salvation, that my whole family believe that Jesus is Lord and by the confession of their mouth and the belief in their heart, we are all saved.

I thank you Lord for being the God that's more than enough, everlasting and omnipotent.

In Jesus Name

OTHER BOOKS BY A REDWOOD THAT CAN BE ORDERED FROM AMAZON

JEZEBEL THE SPIRIT OF MANIPULATION AND WITCHCRAFT

40 DAYS TO CHANGE

INTERCESSORY SERIES Pt.2

HOW TO WALK IN THE PLACE WHERE NOTHING IS IMPOSSIBLE

THE CRUCIFIED SEED

FREE GIFT CALLED HEALING

HEAING SCRIPTURES OF THE BIBLE

A REDWOOD

Liberty Temple Full Gospel Ministries

Chicago, Il 60620

Made in United States
Troutdale, OR
05/13/2025